Plan in a Can!™
All About Birds!
3rd Grade

Full-Day Emergency Sub Plans

by Eve Drueke

Find more ready-made lesson plans from Eve Drueke at Amazon.com

Check out even more original learning materials, games,
and printable books at www.myplaninacan.com.

How to Use Plan in a Can!

Use **Plan in a Can!** when you're...

sick and need a sub	...out for workshops or meetings	...or tired of the same old materials!

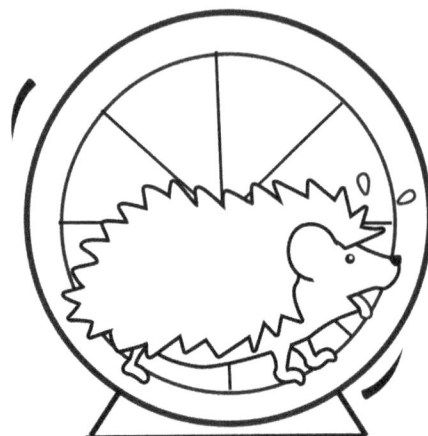

All you have to do is...

1. Make copies using the Copyroom Quick Guide.	2. Take a moment to indicate your preferences for the substitute.	3. Relax! You're done!

Enjoy the peace of mind of knowing your students are engaged in high-interest, meaningful learning activities from **Plan in a Can!**

Plan in a Can!: Third Grade: All About Birds!

Table of Contents

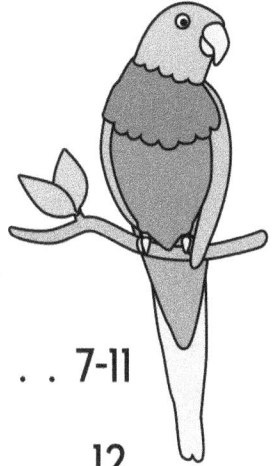

*not numbered in sequence with rest of packet for presentation purposes

© Eve Drueke 2015

A Note from Eve Drueke

Dear Educator,

Thank you so much for your purchase of **Plan in a Can! 3rd Grade: All About Birds**!

If you're like I am, you've spent too many evenings preparing plans before a sick day or teachers' workshop, wishing you already had a set of ready-made lessons to leave for a substitute. At last, I created plans that are clear, ready to use, and full of engaging content and learning activities. Everything is already done for you, including directions for substitute teachers, answer keys, and even helpful forms about vital classroom information for you to fill out, if you choose. If you're in a real pinch, there's even a **Copyroom Checklist** to indicate which activities you need to have copied.

Plan in a Can! includes many printables and activities that can be used again and again. Your purchase entitles you to unlimited use within your own classroom. Please, respect my work and follow copyright law by refraining from distributing these materials outside of your classroom.

I hope you find this ready-made kit useful, engaging, and time-saving! Extra time is a precious commodity in a teacher's life--enjoy getting a little back by opening a **Plan in a Can!**

Many more of my original lesson plans, activities, and mini books are available online at:

Amazon.com
myplaninacan.com
teacherspayteachers.com/Store/Eve-Perlman

Thank you again for your purchase.

Happy Teaching!

Eve Drueke

Important Classroom Information

Vital Information

Emergency procedures and information can be found:

_____

Please note the following students with medical conditions:

Student	Condition	Notes

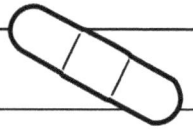

Important Phone Numbers:

Main Office	
Nurse	

Additional Notes

_____

_____

_____

_____

Our Morning Routine:

☐ Students will come in on their own. ☐ Pick students up from _____ at: ___ : ___

When students enter the classroom, they should:

_____

_____

_____

_____

Take attendance by:

_____

_____

Take lunch count by:

_____

_____

Classroom Management:

Our classroom discipline plan:

_____

_____

_____

_____

Extra-reliable students include:

_____

_____

Students who may need additional support following classroom expectations include:

_____

_____

Schedule Details

The following students will leave the classroom:

Student	Time	Destination	Notes

End of Day Procedures

☐ _____

☐ _____

☐ _____

☐ _____

☐ _____

☐ _____

Before you leave, please:

_____

_____

Additional Notes:

_____

_____

_____

_____

Today's Schedule: _____

Time	Activity	Notes

Plan in a Can! 3rd Grade: Lesson Plans

A. Incredible Hummingbirds Book
In the following activity, students will read a book about hummingbirds and answer comprehension questions.

1. Incredible Hummingbirds should be read (choose one):

    ☐ independently   ☐ with partners   ☐ in small groups with your direct guidance

    ☐ in small student-led groups   ☐ as a whole class

2. Distribute the copies of Incredible Hummingbirds.

3. Briefly "walk through" the book with students to preview images and chapter headings. Prompt students to share any predictions about what they will learn as they read.

Students who may require additional support: _____

Additional Notes: _____

_____

B. Incredible Hummingbirds Reading Comprehension Sheets

Once they are finished reading, students should answer questions on the comprehension sheet. Students should refer back to the passage for information.

1. Please distribute (choose from the options below):

Incredible Hummingbirds Comprehension Sheet 1:

☐ to all students   ☐ to the following students: _____

Incredible Hummingbirds Comprehension Sheet 2:

☐ to all students   ☐ to the following students: _____

Students who may require additional support: _____

Additional Notes: _____

_____

C. Incredible Hummingbirds Mini Book

In this activity, students will create their own "mini books", using information they learned by reading Incredible Hummingbirds.

1. Students should keep their copies of Incredible Hummingbirds.

2. Distribute the copies of Incredible Hummingbirds Mini Book.

3. Briefly review and discuss the blank mini book with the students.

4. Guide the students to compare the mini book's page titles to the chapter titles of Incredible Hummingbirds. Note that the titles are the same.

5. Inform the students that on each page of their mini book, they will write and illustrate an important idea (in a full sentence) from the corresponding book chapter.

6. You may want to discuss a possible sentence and illustration as a whole class. View the illustration below for your own knowledge.

Nifty Nests
A mother hummingbird builds her nest in a safe place. She will make her nest high off the ground and hidden behind leaves. A hummingbird nest is safer when snakes or large birds cannot see it. A mother hummingbird uses soft things to make her nest. She uses moss, cotton fluff, and soft plants. She holds the nest together with sticky spider webs!

Photo: Two hummingbird babies peek out of their nest as they wait for their mother to return. Photo by XX XXX

9

Nifty Nests

Hummingbirds use spider webs in their nests.

Students read important ideas here...and write about one of them here.

7. Note that the chapters start with "Fantastic Flyers".

8. Please remind students to write neatly and try to use their own words.

9. Illustrations can be completed (choose one):

☐ after writing   ☐ in any order   ☐ in crayon   ☐ in marker   ☐ in colored pencil

10. Allow students to work until _____ : _____

11. Students may cut and assemble books with their scissors and two staples.

12. Completed mini-books should be: _____

13. Unfinished work should be kept: _____

Additional Notes: _____

_____

_____

D. Independent Reading Book Response

In this activity, students will read their chapter books (novels) independently, and then respond to the book using the Independent Reading Book Response Sheet.

1. Distribute the Independent Reading Book Response sheets.

2. Inform students that while they read quietly in their books for _____ minutes, they will respond by answering prompts on the Independent Reading Response Sheet.

3. Discuss each section of the worksheet. (You may want to display or distribute the illustrated guide on how to use the book response sheet, found on page 14.)

4. Each section should be completed as follows:
a. I ❤ This Part: Students should write 1-2 sentences about a part of their reading they really enjoyed (and explain why).
b. I Have a Prediction: Students should write down what they think may happen next, at the end of their reading.
c. I Have Some Questions: Students can write down 1-2 questions about anything that is confusing, or general questions about the story, such as, "I wonder why the girl is so mean," or "Could the neighbor's dog be the one digging holes in the park?"
d. This Made a Big Impression: Here, students record anything they thought was surprising, amazing, scary, funny, or memorable.
e. I See a Connection: students write down any similarities they see between their book and any other literature or events. For example, "This reminds me of an Ivy and Bean book, because both books have girls that have to solve problems at school".

5. Completed work should be placed:_____

Additional Notes: _____

E. Spelling Practice: Monkey on My Back

In this activity, students practice their weekly Spelling words with a partner, using a fun "Monkey Sheet".

1. Inform students that they will be practicing their Spelling words with partners, using a fun activity called "Monkey On My Back". Explain to students that the term "monkey on my back" refers to something that's bothersome or a burden, especially for a long period of time. For example, you might say, "My mom makes me rake leaves every Saturday before I can go play. That chore is a real monkey on my back!"

9

2. Explain that sometimes, not knowing Spelling words (especially if there's a test coming up), can feel like having a monkey on your back, too. With today's activity, students will practice their Spelling words, and thus, get the monkeys off their backs.

3. Students should begin with a copy of this week's Spelling words, a partner, a pencil, and a Monkey Sheet.

4. Partner 1 gives Partner 2 a word to spell. Partner 2 must correctly spell the word aloud while Partner 1 checks the spelling from the list. If Partner 2 spells the word correctly, he or she gets to cross one monkey off his or her sheet. If Partner 2 spells the word wrong, he or she cannot cross off a monkey, but should instead copy their word onto the Monkey Sheet for additional practice later.

5. Repeat Step 4 until one partner crosses off all the monkeys from his or her sheet. Students who spelled words incorrectly should take their monkey sheets home for review.

Additional Notes: _____

F. ABC Chart

In this activity, students will fill out an alphabetical chart with vocabulary words or other important terms from a selection of reading.

1. Distribute the two-sided ABC Chart. Inform students that after reading in their _____ books, they will show what they've learned by recording important information in their ABC Charts.

2. Students should read pages _____ in their _____ books.

3. Students should read (choose one):

☐ independently   ☐ with partners   ☐ in small groups   ☐ as a whole class

4. After students have completed reading, they should begin completing the chart with important terms from the reading.

5. Students should complete at least ____ squares on the chart.

6. See sample on following page.

Additional Notes: _____

A air pressure is the weight of air pressing on earth	B barometers are tools that measure air pressure	C cumulus clouds are large, fluffy, and high in the sky
D dew is water that forms on objects close to the ground	E evaporation happens when a liquid changes to a vapor	F

G. Math: Area Practice

1. Distribute the Math Practice: Area sheet. 1. It should be completed by (choose one):

☐ all students   ☐ the following students: _____

_____

2. Briefly cover directions from the sheet and the example.
3. Remind students to show their work and label units.
4. Students may not use calculators.
5. Completed work should be placed: _____

H. Math: Area Challenge Word Problems

The Math: Area Challenge Word Problems should be (choose one):

☐ done by all students   ☐ available for early-finishers   ☐ other:_____

Additional Notes:_____

I. Math: Rainbow Lorikeet Multiplication Color-by-Number

Students should complete the multiplication problems and color each section the correct color, according to the key. They may not use calculators.

When finished, students should place the multiplication sheets:_____

Additional Notes:_____

Plan in a Can: 3rd Grade: All About Birds!
Copyroom Quick Guide

Make Copies of the Following:

Number of Copies:

Independent Reading Book Response
1 Page

Monkey On My Back Spelling Practice
1 Page, 2 Per Game Cards Per Sheet

Spelling Lists: 1 Regular, 1 Challenge
1 Page

ABC Chart for Content Area
2 Pages, Back to Back

Math Area Practice
1 Page

Math Area Word Problem Challenge
1 Page

Rainbow Lorikeet Multiplication Practice
1 Page

Hummingbird Comprehension Sheet 1 (short answer)
1 Page

Hummingbird Comprehension Sheet 2 (multiple choice)
1 Page

Incredible Hummingbirds Printable Book
9 Pages

Incredible Hummingbirds Mini Book
4 Pages

Also Copy:

Independent Reading Book Response

Reader:_____

Title of Book:_____   Pages Read Today:_____

I ♡ This Part!	
I have a 🔍 prediction...	
I have some ❓ questions.	
This made a ✸ BIG impression!	
I see a 🧩 connection.	

Independent Reading Book Response

Reader: <u>Sample</u>

Title of Book: <u>Because of Winn Dixie</u>   Pages Read Today: <u>2</u> — <u>10</u>

I ♥ This Part!	I just love when Opal meets the stray dog at a grocery store! I love dogs and it would be so funny to see one at a store.
I have a prediction...	I predict that Opal and the dog will be friends. Opal seems lonely and the dog doesn't have an owner.
I have some ? questions.	Why didn't Opal's mother move with Opal and her father? Why does her father have church in an old store?
This made a BIG impression!	I am going to remember the part where the dog runs around the grocery store, upsetting everyone, especially the manager! I think it was brave and kind of Opal to say the stray dog was hers.
I see a connection.	So far, this story reminds me of the book <u>James and the Giant Peach</u>, because they are both about children who feel very lonely.

14

Monkey On My Back Game Sheets

Player:

Words to Practice:

_____

_____

_____

_____

Player:

Words to Practice:

_____

_____

_____

_____

15

Spelling: Common Sight Words and Challenge List

Spelling List: Common Sight Words

1. laugh
2. light
3. eight
4. together
5. would
6. could
7. people
8. where
9. were
10. these
11. again
12. great
13. they
14. other
15. another

Name: _____

Challenge List: Commonly Misspelled Words

1. arctic
2. paid
3. believe
4. argue
5. principal
6. women
7. writing
8. usual
9. control
10. February
11. surprise
12. changing
13. until
14. maybe
15. ninety

Name: _____

The ABC's of: _____ By: _____

A	B	C
D	E	F
G	H	I
J	K	L

M	N	O
P	Q	R
S	T	U
V	W/X	Y/Z

18

Math Practice: Area

Name: _____

Find the area of the rectangles below.
Be sure to show your work and label units.

Example:

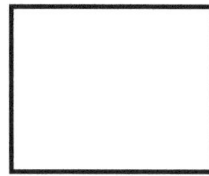

4 in

5 in

5 x 4 = 20

20 inches²

- -

1.)

3 feet

6 feet

_____

2.)

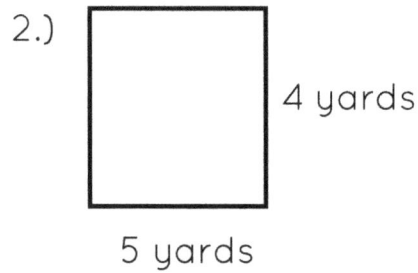

4 yards

5 yards

_____

3.)

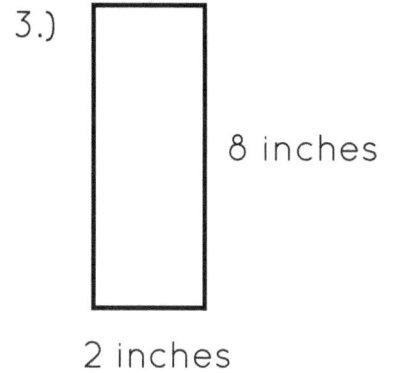

8 inches

2 inches

_____

4.)

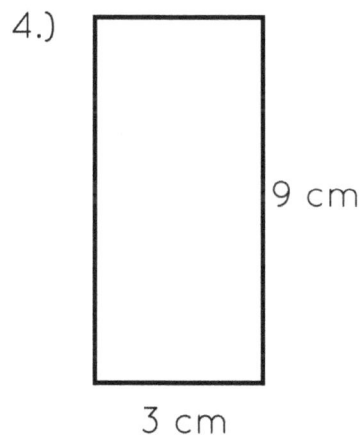

9 cm

3 cm

_____

5.)

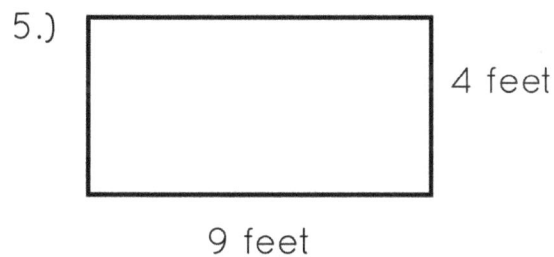

4 feet

9 feet

_____

6.)

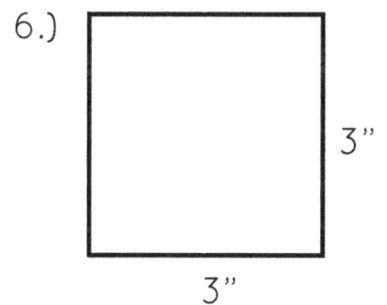

3"

3"

_____

7.)

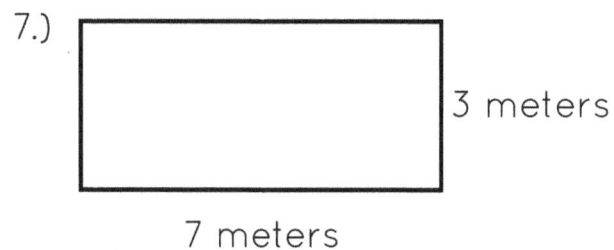

3 meters

7 meters

_____

8.)

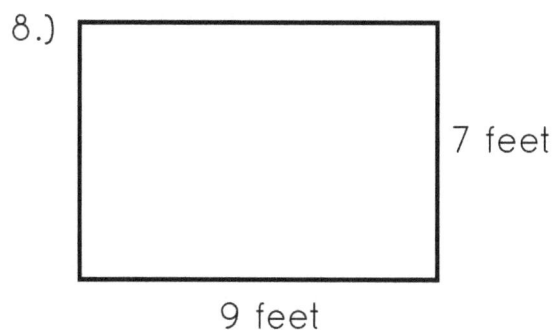

7 feet

9 feet

_____

19

Math: Area Word Problem Challenge

Name: _____

Read each problem and solve. Be sure to show your work and label units.
Circle your answer.

1. Zookeepers are making a space for the new baby ostrich to run. The plans for the space are below. What is the area of the new ostrich's space?

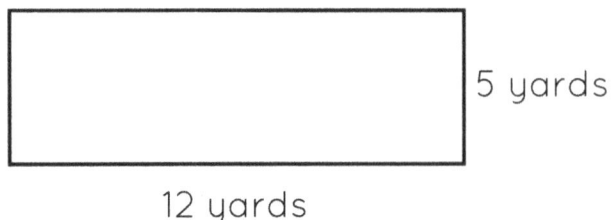

5 yards

12 yards

2. Alex is planting a flower garden for hummingbirds. The garden is 4 feet wide. It is twice as long as is is wide. How many square feet is Alex's garden?

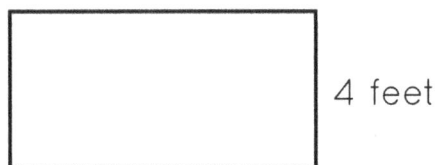

4 feet

3. The hawk sanctuary is 12 miles long by 8 miles wide. What is the total area of the sanctuary?

4. Below is a drawing of the bridge over the penguin pool at the aquarium. What is the total area of the bridge?

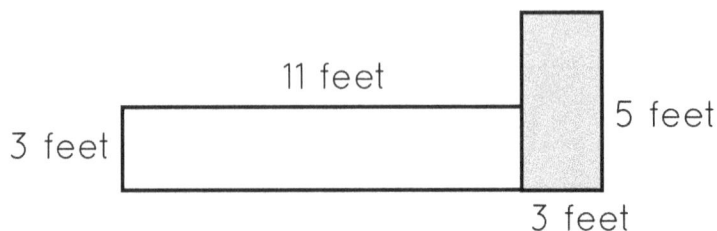

11 feet

5 feet

3 feet

3 feet

5. The third grade planted a prairie garden to help feed wild birds. The total area of the garden is 48 feet. It is 8 feet long. How wide is the garden?

20

Rainbow Lorikeet Color-by-Number

Name: _____

Fill in the blanks. Use the key to color.

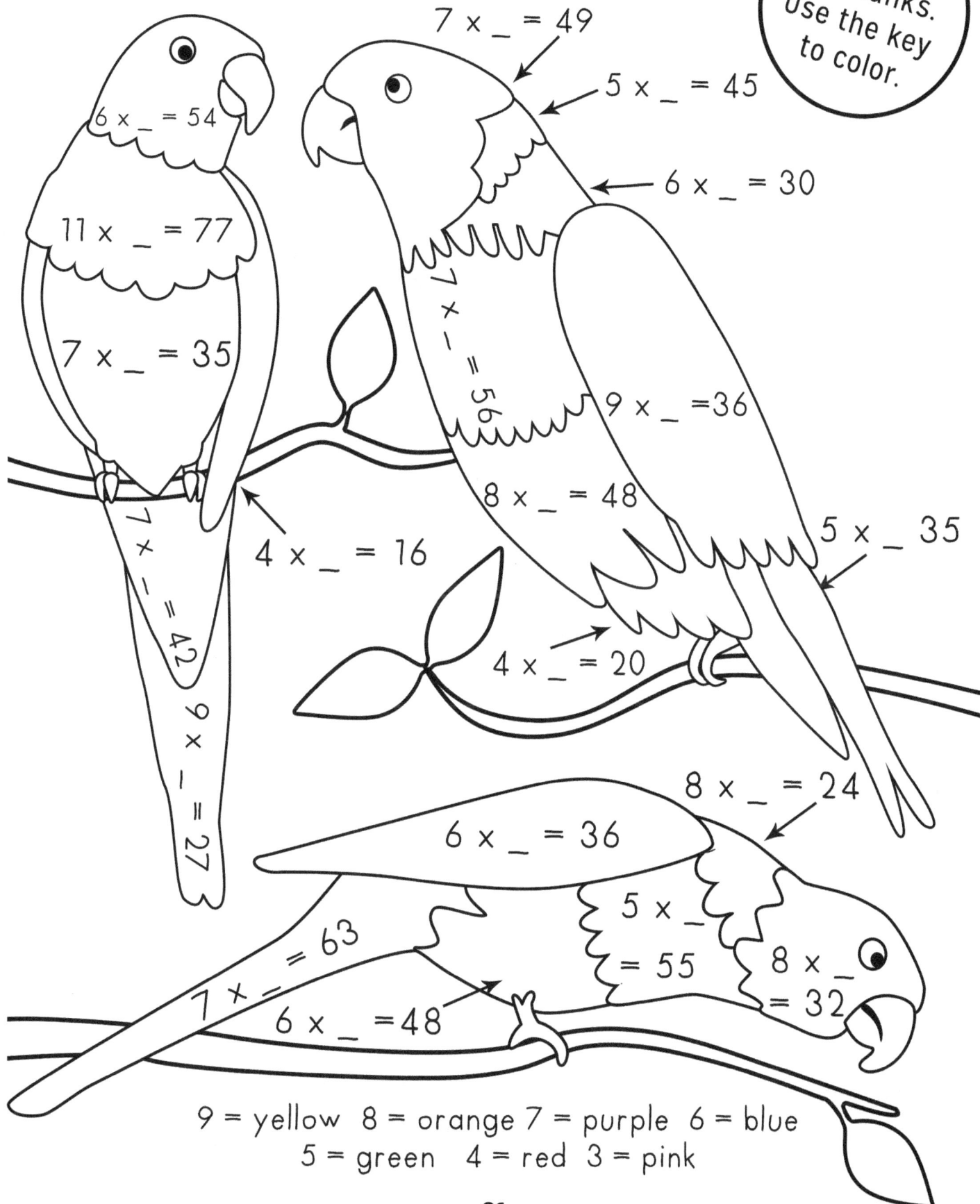

$6 \times \_ = 54$

$7 \times \_ = 49$

$5 \times \_ = 45$

$6 \times \_ = 30$

$11 \times \_ = 77$

$7 \times \_ = 56$

$7 \times \_ = 35$

$9 \times \_ = 36$

$8 \times \_ = 48$

$4 \times \_ = 16$

$5 \times \_ 35$

$7 \times \_ = 42$

$4 \times \_ = 20$

$9 \times \_ = 27$

$8 \times \_ = 24$

$6 \times \_ = 36$

$5 \times \_ = 55$

$8 \times \_ = 32$

$7 \times \_ = 63$

$6 \times \_ = 48$

9 = yellow 8 = orange 7 = purple 6 = blue
5 = green   4 = red 3 = pink

21

© Eve Drueke 2015

Incredible Hummingbirds!: Comprehension Check 1

Reader: _____

Use the book <u>Incredible Hummingbirds!</u> to answer the questions below.
Answer in full sentences. Use the back if you need more space.

1. Hummingbirds can fly in ways that other birds can't. What are these ways?

1: _____

2: _____

2. List two ways that one species of hummingbird can look different from other species of hummingbirds.

1: _____

2: _____

3. Explain how a hummingbird's beak and tongue help it drink nectar.

_____

_____

4. List two things in a hummingbird's diet.

_____

_____

5. How do most hummingbirds get ready for a long migration South?

_____

_____

6. Name two things that mother hummingbirds provide for their babies.

_____

_____

7. Describe one way humans can help hummingbirds.

_____

Incredible Hummingbirds!: Comprehension Check 2

Reader:_____

Use the book <u>Incredible Hummingbirds!</u> to answer the questions below.

1. Name two special ways that hummingbirds can fly:

a. _____   b. _____

2. Name two things that can be different about hummingbirds' bodies.

a. _____   b. _____

3. A hummingbird uses its _____ and _____
to reach nectar inside flowers.

4. Name three things a hummingbird eats.

a. _____   b. _____

c. _____

5. Most hummingbirds get ready to migrate South by:

◯ a. sleeping a lot   ◯ b. eating extra food   ◯ c. making nests

6. Name two things mother hummingbirds give their new babies.

a. _____   b. _____

7. One way humans can help hummingbirds is:

_____

Read & Discover:
Incredible Hummingbirds!

3rd Grade and Up!

a non-fiction book by Eve Drueke

Read & Discover:
Incredible Hummingbirds!
by Eve Drueke

Discover more books, games, and learning materials from Eve Drueke
on Amazon.com and myplaninacan.com!

Special Hummingbirds

Some animals are special because of their large size, sharp teeth, or strong bodies. Did you know the tiny hummingbird is a very special animal too? These small birds are incredible in many ways. Read on to find out why the little hummingbird is a big deal!

Photo: A hummingbird flies to a flower to stop for food.

Fantastic Flyers

Hummingbirds are experts at flying. They can hover in one place, fly backwards, or even fly upside down! Hummingbirds flap their wings at a very high speed. When their wings move quickly, they make a low humming sound. This sound is where hummingbirds get their name.

Photo: A Purple-Throated Carib hummingbird hovers in the air and drinks from a flower. Credit: Charles J. Sharp

Hummingbirds Are Different

There are about 340 kinds of hummingbirds in the world. In North America, hummingbirds can be found from Alaska to Mexico during the summer months. Most **species** of hummingbirds live in Central America and South America. Hummingbirds have different

A Bee Hummingbird is only about 2 inches tall when it is an adult. Its eggs are the size of tiny jelly beans! Illustration: Eve Drueke

colors, sizes, and beaks. The largest hummingbird is called the Giant Hummingbird. It is about 5 inches tall. The smallest hummingbird is called the Bee Hummingbird. It is only 5 centimeters high when it is an adult!

Beaks Are Tools

Hummingbirds have special beaks. Their beaks are long, thin, and curved. A humming-bird's beak helps it reach nectar deep inside flowers. Hummingbirds drink sweet and sticky nectar for food. Hummingbirds' tongues also help them drink nectar. Their tongues are long and skinny and have tiny tubes on the side. These tubes help nectar flow into a hummingbird's mouth.

Photo: A hummingbird uses its long beak to reach the nectar deep inside a flower.

Food Is Fuel

Hummingbirds use lots of energy when they fly. They have to eat plenty of food each day to have enough energy to live. Hummingbirds eat more than nectar. Their diet includes insects and spiders. When a hummingbird finds something good to eat, it may try to chase other hummingbirds away so it can have all of the food to itself.

Photo: a young female Ruby-throated Hummingbird sips nectar from a beebalm flower.

6

- -

Hummingbirds Need Heat

Hummingbirds are too small to survive in cold winters. They must find a warm place to live when the weather gets cold. Most hummingbirds **migrate** to reach Central or South America and fly without stopping! Because hummingbirds need so much energy to fly for a long time, they will eat plenty of extra food before leaving for a long trip South.

United States

Mexico

Gulf of Mexico

Belize
Honduras
Guatemala
Nicaragua
El Salvador
Costa Rica
Panama

Most hummingbirds in the United States migrate to Mexico and Central America. Some fly as far south as Panama and travel over the Gulf of Mexico without land to stop and rest!

7

Hummingbirds Are Helpers

Something special happens when a hummingbird drinks from a flower. Like bees and butterflies, humming-birds help **pollinate** flowers. Hummingbirds will pick up a tiny bit of pollen from inside the flower. The hummingbird will leave a little pollen on the next flower it visits. Flowers need pollen to make new seeds and new flowers grow.

Photo: A hummingbird has pollen on its beak after drinking nectar from a flower. Photo by Kpts44

8

Nifty Nests

A mother hummingbird builds her nest in a safe place. She will make her nest high off the ground and hidden behind leaves. A hummingbird nest is safer when snakes or large birds cannot see it. A mother hummingbird uses soft things to make her nest. She uses moss, **lichen**, cotton fluff, and soft plants. She holds the nest together with sticky spider webs!

Photo: Two hummingbird babies peek out of their nest as they wait for their mother to return.

9

Itty Bitty Babies

Hummingbirds lay two tiny white eggs. The eggs will hatch in about 18 days. Baby hummingbirds are very tiny. They are so small, they weigh less than a dime! When baby hummingbirds first hatch, they have no feathers and cannot see.

Photo: A hummingbird feeds her two babies. This hummingbird lives in South America. It makes a nest that hangs.

They need their mother to feed them and keep them safe and warm.

10

Incredible Birds

Hummingbirds are special in many ways. They can fly in ways that other birds cannot. They have special beaks for drinking nectar. Hummingbirds can even help flowers grow. What do you think makes hummingbirds so incredible?

Photo: A hummingbird sips nectar for energy.

11

You Can Help Hummingbirds!

Here are some ways to help hummingbirds:

1. Plant flowers that hummingbirds like.
2. Hang up a hummingbird feeder and fill it with hummingbird food.
3. Plant trees and bushes to give hummingbirds a safe place to make their nests.

Photo: An Anna's hummingbird sits at a feeder filled with a special sugar water drink.

4. Do not use poisonous bug sprays around your home. Birds might eat insects with poison on them and get very sick or die!

12

Here are some flowers you can plant to help hummingbirds.

**Photos:
Left: sage by Oswald Engelhard, top right: columbine by Peter Ruhr, bottom right: butterfly bush by Sage Ross.**

13

Hummingbird Nectar

You can make this sugar water mixture at home to feed local hummingbirds.
BE SURE TO HAVE AN ADULT HELP YOU WHEN USING THE STOVE.

1 cup tap water
¼ cup granulated white sugar

Bring tap water to a boil and stir in the sugar. Stir until the sugar is dissolved. Allow mixture to cool to room temperature before adding it to your hummingbird feeder. To make bigger portions, mix 1 part sugar to 4 parts water. The mixture will keep in the refrigerator for up to two weeks.

Do not use food coloring, honey, brown sugar, unrefined sugar or sugar substitutes. These can be very harmful to hummingbirds. Never, ever use insecticides or other poisons at hummingbird feeders.

14

- -

Glossary

lichen (LIKE-en): fungus that grows along with algae. Lichen is often green, gray, yellow, or black and looks a flake or bit of leaf. Lichen often grows on branches or rocks.

migrate: to move from one place or climate to another

pollinate: to move pollen from plant to plant

species: a kind of type of living thing

15

Incredible Hummingbirds!

A Mini Non-Fiction Book By:

_____

Fantastic Flyers:

_____
_____
_____

2

Incredible Hummingbirds!

This book is dedicated to:

_____

© Eve Drueke 2015

Hummingbirds Are Different:

_____
_____
_____

3

Beaks Are Tools:

Food Is Fuel:

Hummingbirds Need Heat:

4

Hummingbirds Are Helpers:

5

6

7

Nifty Nests:

Itty Bitty Babies:

You Can Help Hummingbirds:

8

9

Incredible Birds:

10

I think hummingbirds are incredible because

11

Math Practice: Area

Name: _Answer Key_

Find the area of the rectangles below.
Be sure to show your work and label units.

Example:

$5 \times 4 = 20$

20 inches^2

4 in

5 in

- -

1.)
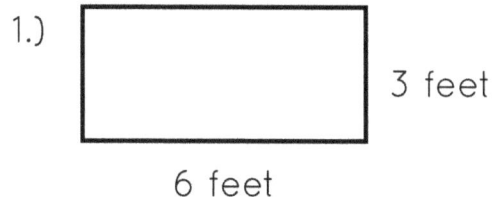
3 feet
6 feet

$\underline{18 \text{ feet}^2}$

2.)
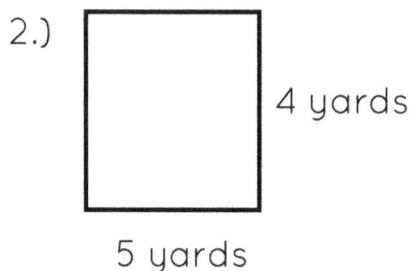
4 yards
5 yards

$\underline{20 \text{ yards}^2}$

3.)
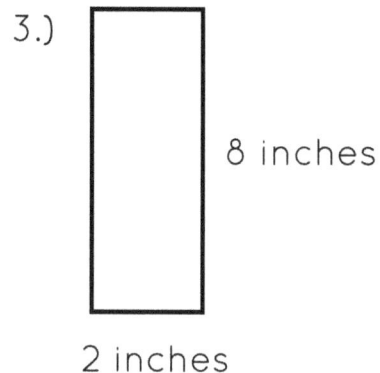
8 inches
2 inches

$\underline{16 \text{ inches}^2}$

4.)
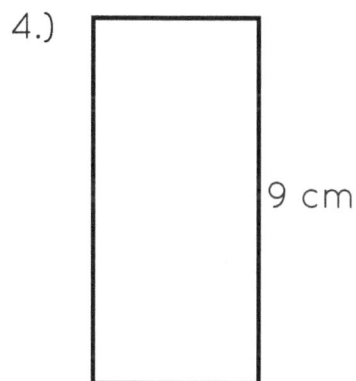
9 cm
3 cm

$\underline{27 \text{ cm}^2}$

5.)
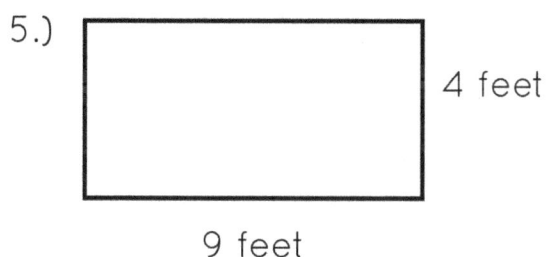
4 feet
9 feet

$\underline{36 \text{ feet}^2}$

6.)
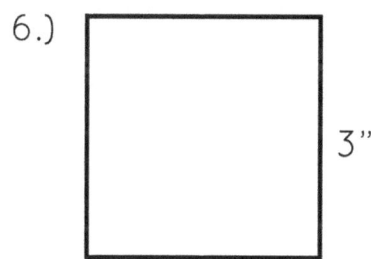
3"
3"

$\underline{9 "^2}$

7.)

3 meters
7 meters

$\underline{21 \text{ meters}^2}$

8.)
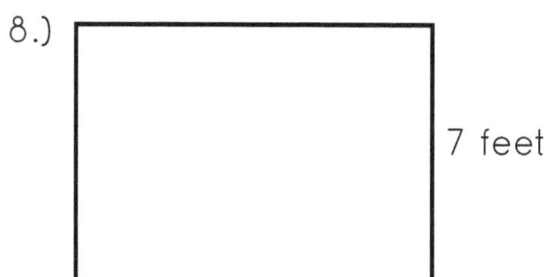
7 feet
9 feet

$\underline{63 \text{ feet}^2}$

24

© Eve Drueke 2015

Math: Area Word Problem Challenge

Name: Answer Key

Read each problem and solve. Be sure to show your work and label units.
Circle your answer.

1. Zookeepers are making a space for the new baby ostrich to run. The plans for the space are below. What is the area of the new ostrich's space?

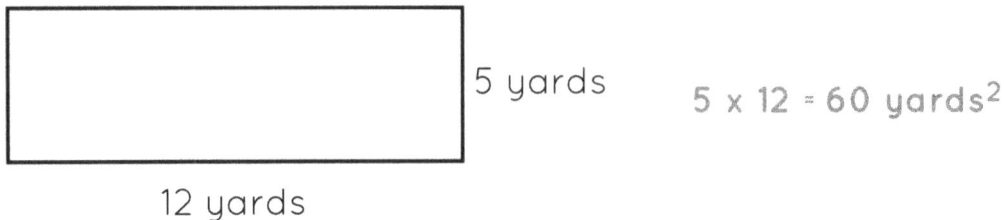

5 yards

12 yards

$5 \times 12 = 60$ yards^2

2. Alex is planting a flower garden for hummingbirds. The garden is 4 feet wide. It is twice as long as is is wide. How many square feet is Alex's garden?

4 feet

8 feet

4 feet x 8 feet

= 32 feet^2

3. The hawk sanctuary is 12 miles long by 8 miles wide. What is the total area of the sanctuary?

$12 \times 8 = 96$ miles^2

4. Below is a drawing of the bridge over the penguin pool at the aquarium. What is the total area of the bridge?

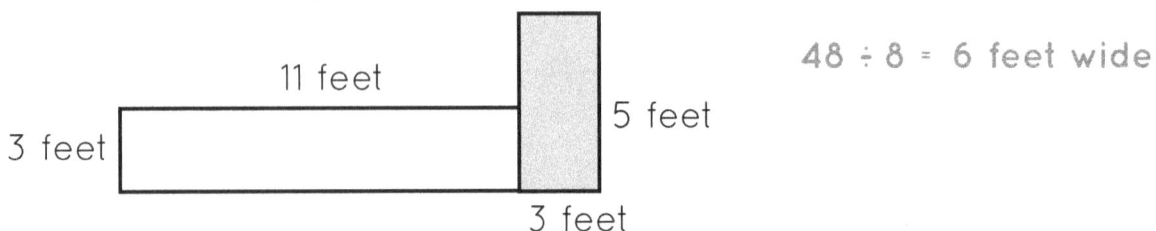

11 feet

3 feet

5 feet

3 feet

$48 \div 8 = 6$ feet wide

5. The third grade planted a prairie garden to help feed wild birds. The total area of the garden is 48 feet. It is 8 feet long. How wide is the garden?

$3 \times 11 = 33$ feet, $5 \times 3 = 15$ feet, $33 + 15 = 48$ feet^2

25

Rainbow Lorikeet Color-by-Number

Name: __Answer Key__

Fill in the blanks. Use the key to color.

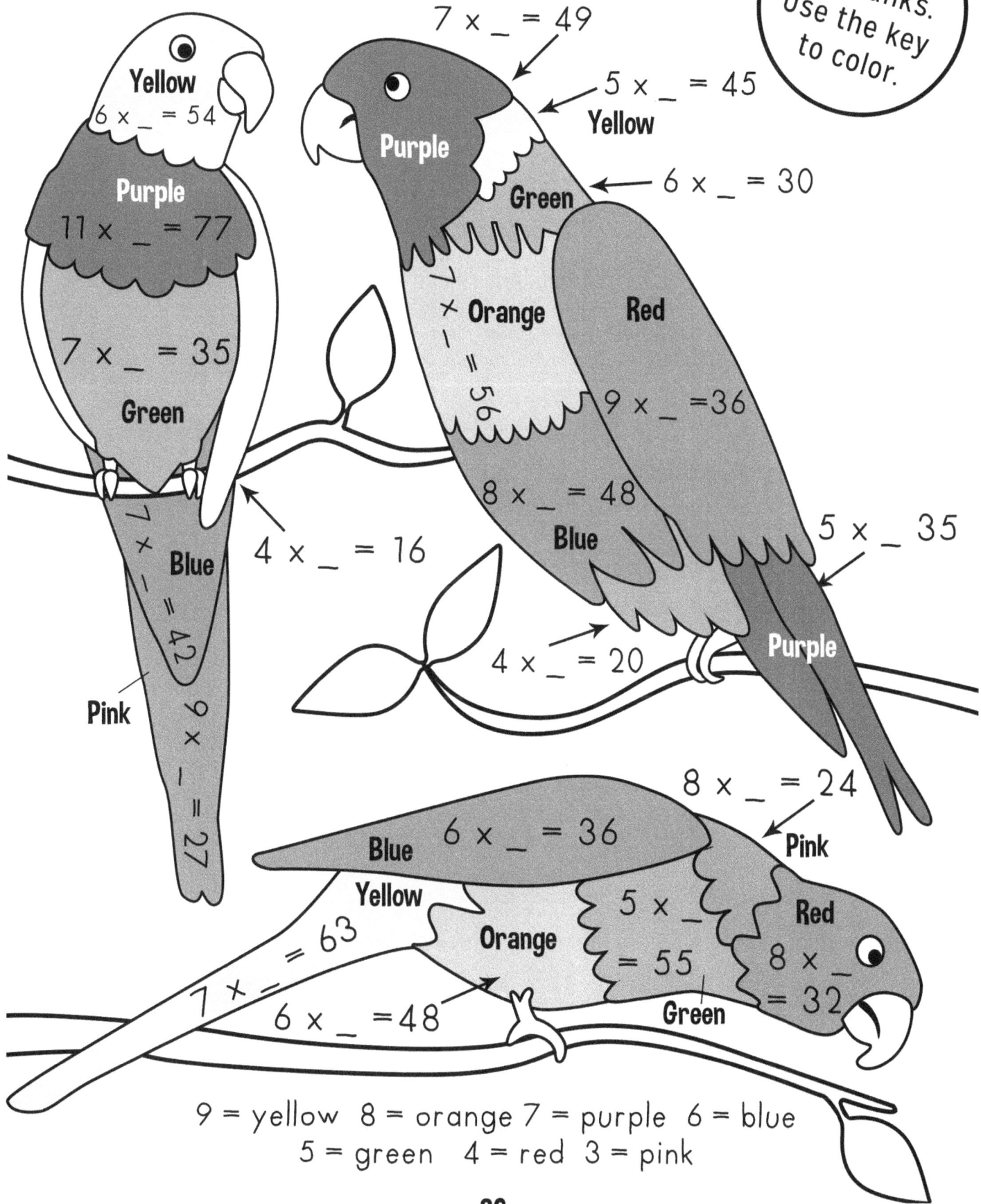

$7 \times \_ = 49$

$5 \times \_ = 45$

Yellow

$6 \times \_ = 30$

Yellow

$6 \times \_ = 54$

Purple

$11 \times \_ = 77$

$7 \times \_ = 35$

Green

Purple

Green

$7 \times \_ = 56$

Orange

Red

$9 \times \_ = 36$

$8 \times \_ = 48$

Blue

$5 \times \_ \ 35$

Purple

$4 \times \_ = 16$

$7 \times \_ = 42$

Blue

Pink

$9 \times \_ = 27$

$4 \times \_ = 20$

$8 \times \_ = 24$

Pink

$6 \times \_ = 36$

Blue

Yellow

Red

$5 \times \_ = 55$

$8 \times \_ = 32$

Orange

Green

$7 \times \_ = 63$

$6 \times \_ = 48$

9 = yellow 8 = orange 7 = purple 6 = blue
5 = green 4 = red 3 = pink

26

© Eve Drueke 2015

Incredible Hummingbirds!: Comprehension Check 1

Reader: **Answer Key**

Use the book <u>Incredible Hummingbirds!</u> to answer the questions below.
Answer in full sentences. Use the back if you need more space.

1. Hummingbirds can fly in ways that other birds can't. What are these ways?

1: Answers include flying backwards or upside down, hovering,

2: and flying at a high speed.

2. List two ways that one species of hummingbird can look different from other species of hummingbirds.

1: Hummingbird species can vary in color, size, and type of bill.

2:

3. Explain how a hummingbird's beak and tongue help it drink nectar.

Hummingbirds' long, narrow beaks help them reach nectar deep inside flowers. Long, thin tongues with small tubes help make the nectar flow into hummingbirds' mouths.

4. List two things in a hummingbird's diet.

Hummingbirds drink nectar, as well as eat insects and spiders.

5. How do most hummingbirds get ready for a long migration South?

Most migratory hummingbirds prepare by eating extra food.

6. Name two things that mother hummingbirds provide for their babies.

Mother hummingbirds provide a nest (shelter/safety), warmth, and food.

7. Describe one way humans can help hummingbirds.

Answers include planting trees and shrubs for habitat, protecting existing habitat, planting flowers that produce nectar, providing artificial food, and avoiding the use of poisons or pesticides.

Incredible Hummingbirds!: Comprehension Check 2

Reader: _Answer Key_

Use the book <u>Incredible Hummingbirds!</u> to answer the questions below.

1. Name two special ways that hummingbirds can fly:

a. _upside down, backwards,_ b. _hovering, or quickly_

2. Name two things that can be different about hummingbirds' bodies.

a. _shape of beak, color,_ b. _or size_

3. A hummingbird uses its _____ beak _____ and _____ tongue _____
to reach nectar inside flowers.

4. Name three things a hummingbird eats.

a. _nectar_ b. _insects_

c. _spiders_ (spiders are not insects, they are arachnids!)

5. Most hummingbirds get ready to migrate South by:

⚪ a. sleeping a lot   ⚫ b. eating extra food   ⚪ c. making nests

6. Name two things mother hummingbirds give their new babies.

a. _shelter/safety, food,_ b. _or warmth_

7. One way humans can help hummingbirds is:

Answers include planting trees and shrubs for habitat, protecting existing habitat, planting flowers that produce nectar, providing artificial food, and avoiding the use of poisons or pesticides.

28

www.ingramcontent.com/pod-product-compliance
Lightning Source LLC
Chambersburg PA
CBHW081233020426
42331CB00012B/3151